EXPLORING THE COUNTRYSIDE

By the Same Author

Good Girl Sesky
Sesky's Farmyard Friends

EXPLORING THE COUNTRYSIDE

The Children's Dynamic Knowledge Book

JANETTE McKEAGUE

Published in 2024 by Dynamic Dream Books

Copyright © Janette McKeague 2024

Janette McKeague has asserted her right to be identified as the author of this Work in accordance with the Copyright, Designs and Patents Act 1988

ISBN Paperback: 978-1-7399475-4-5
Ebook: 978-1-7399475-5-2

All rights reserved. No part of this publication may be reproduced, stored in a retrieval system, or transmitted in any form or by any means, electronic, mechanical, photocopying, recording or otherwise, without the prior permission of the copyright owner.

A CIP catalogue copy of this book can be found in the British Library.

Published with the help of Indie Authors World
www.indieauthorsworld.com

I dedicate this book to all the children who love the magnificent countryside, nature and the animals and to those of you who soon will.

Let's go and explore, from farmers to animals and birds and much more.

This book belongs to:

_____

Introduction

The Children's Dynamic Knowledge Book

Welcome to your book, Exploring the Countryside.

In this book, farmer Shaki (also known as Davey) and I will show you and tell you about our magnificent countryside and the environment, including its animals and land. We will explain how he and the other farmers look after the land and provide a food source for their animals, for you, and everyone else.

Follow us as we harvest grass, food, and the crops grown on the land, and you will discover how much of it ends up in the food chain, then moves into the shops for sale or for us to buy directly from the farmers, and then eventually ends up on your plate for you to eat.

The animals we breed to provide food, from milk and eggs to the meat you eat, are all part of this exciting journey.

With our fantastic, friendly countryside animals and a few things that help save the environment and are good for the planet, we will keep you guessing what is coming next.

As you turn the pages, you will gain more knowledge and discover what keeps the countryside rolling and our animals moving, including our magnificent birds of prey flying over the land.

A farmer's work is never-ending, and tomorrow is always just another day.

Enjoy your dynamic book.

Janette and Shaki

Chapter 1

The Countryside - Changing Seasons

As the long, dark nights and short days of winter give way to February, the days start to get lighter and longer, and we can sigh with relief that spring is not too far away and everything seems brighter.

Have you ever thought about the countryside and how beautiful it is? With our stunning Scottish scenery, hills, mountains, and lochs, there are so many enchanting colours and surprises that are just waiting to be found.

Each year, we have four seasons: spring, summer, autumn, and winter. As we move through these seasons, the colours of the countryside change, and every month tells a different story as it holds onto its time.

With spring starting off the seasons again, fresh blossoms and colours arise out of the darkened months of winter.

Young shoots appear in the soil as if reaching for the sky. The earth softens beneath your feet as you walk across the fields where the cold winter frost and snow have melted.

Fresh green grass shoots through the ground as if the blue sky is calling down and encouraging it to grow.

The sun appears, and its glittering rays gradually warm the air. Birds gather and sing their song as they fly about more in the brighter skies.

Trees regain their strength and look like they are coming to life as their fresh shoots grow. Within no time at all, new green leaves appear. The branches reach far and wide again as if opening up to the sky, and the emptiness of the space that once lay on the tree's branches through the winter months is once again filled with colour.

The hedge lines fill out and align the barrier to the fields, which once stood thin and gaping. As the first glittering snowdrops appear from the ground, followed by the beauty of the yellow spread of daffodils, you know spring has sprung.

Sometimes, it makes you wonder what all the winter darkness and cold months are about and why we can't just hold onto spring and summer forever!

The great things about the countryside that draw many of us to it are its big, wide-open spaces and the beauty that lies within. This might be having a great walk or drive for the whole family or, if you're fortunate enough, riding a horse or pony in these magnificent places. Seeing the selection of the birds chirping and flying and the freedom of the animals roaming around just makes you want to see more.

The countryside is where you can be close to and see the beauty of nature with the stunning scenery, views of the fields, trees, and never-ending land. If you stroll far enough, you could disappear into a world of beauty and recreation. City streets and noisy cars can be left behind as you experience the quietness of nature and the unknown surprises that the countryside unfolds as you stroll along and explore the different parts, leading to the beauty within the countryside.

The farmers play a big part in the countryside, looking after their land all year and working hard to keep everything turning over. As Shaki would say, never a day goes by without another job needing to be done. Then he gets his diggers out and starts turning his hand to lots of different jobs and multi-tasking again.

One of Shaki's important jobs is to deal with the drainage throughout the fields, keeping it working so the ground doesn't flood and it stays good for the animals, the crops and for the farmers to work on. It also helps to keep the soil healthy, with the wildlife still being able to use the fields without coming to any harm.

Shaki says that, if possible, it is more environmentally friendly to fix these field drains with the original underground clay piping rather than putting plastic-type drainage pipes into the ground. Also, broken bits of old clay pipes left in the soil don't cause any harm to the earth. This method helps to keep our soil and fields in good condition.

Looking after these drains and ditches is vital so the water doesn't flood from them into the fields, roads, or pathways, which helps keep the environment safe and clean. These drains save the fields from becoming waterlogged and turning into mud baths, which in return can cause damage to the soil and kill the crops and their roots.

Shaki cleans the ditches

The experience of smelling newly cut grass in spring and summer is one not to be missed. After the farmers cut the grass, the fields change colour for a while, leaving a fantastic smell lingering in the air as the farmers make silage, haylage and hay for feeding their animals.

For a while, a slight tint of yellow lies across the fields until the new fresh grass re-grows again to start the procedure all over again in some of the fields. As the animals enjoy grazing on the rest, Shaki and the other farmers get on with many other jobs that need to be done throughout the year.

If you walk up a hill, you can get a bird's-eye view, and you will see far across the land for miles and all the different colours. Where the fields have been worked on and ploughed, this looks dark and just like dirt for a while before being re-sown with fresh seed or crops. Other fields might be different shades of green as the grass grows.

You can also see the animals spread across the land from up on a hill. Stand there, take it all in, daydreaming that the summer months could stay all year.

But as incredible and beautiful as summer is, remember that nature leads us through the months and seasons every year like magic.

You get this magnificent view over Loch Lomond and the surrounding area at the top of Duncryne Hill in Gartocharn, known as The Dumpling.

Did you know?

Duncryne Hill (or The Dumpling as it's known) is a small hill standing only 465 feet above sea level. It is said to have been formed millions of years ago as a volcano. To get to the top is a good climb, but it doesn't take too long. You can follow a pathway through a small tree area, then over fields and up the track to the top of the hill for magnificent views over the surrounding land as you walk. Once you reach the top, you can see the beautiful Loch Lomond with breathtaking views of this wonderful loch, the islands within it, and the surrounding scenery. On clear days, the views of Ben Lomond, Ben Arthur (The Cobbler), and Ben Vorlich are worth seeing. Maybe one of these could be your next climb.

The Dumpling is a lovely little hill, but I don't think it looks much like the dumpling cake you may know.

The beautiful colours of the countryside constantly change throughout the different seasons, from strong green colours in the spring and summer to the yellow golden-brown colours in the autumn. When the temperature is cooler and the rain begins to fall more, the leaves fall to the ground, and you get that crunchy, crisp sound as you walk over them. The trees gradually become bare once more. The fields become lighter in colour as the grass dies off with the turning of the seasons. Even when we know the darker days will be approaching with the wetter, colder, frosty, snowy days and nights, these fields, countryside, and animals will still be looked after by Shaki and the other hard-working farmers because the weather and seasons never bring any rest for them.

Chapter 2

Countryside Wonders and Our Farmers

When you are out walking or driving in the countryside, you may come across or see horse riders enjoying the beauty of the countryside. Riding a horse or a pony is another way to experience this wonderful sense of freedom and enjoy the open space we can all find.

As the horse and rider might not see what is ahead of them or around the corner, it is always wise to take care in the countryside. Pass animals carefully; while walking, have any dogs on the lead in case of sudden animal reactions. Find areas where it is safe to allow the dogs to run free so they can enjoy the freedom of the countryside with you.

Although horses and ponies are ridden on the roads as they need to get to different places, in some parts of the countryside, there are dedicated paths called bridle paths or bridleways, depending on where you are.

These are specially made as safe off-road paths for horse and pony riders, helping them to ride freely without being on the roads with any traffic and hazards while enjoying a variety of ground to cover as they ride at different and faster paces.

If you venture onto these, be aware that you may find a horse or a group of them galloping towards you!

You will see a wide range of animals happily grazing in the fields. Some will be together as a group, and others will be split into different fields. The farmers rotate the animals in the fields to help with the production of good grass and food for the animals. Sheep will eat away the parts of the grass that the cows and horses won't eat. Having sheep grazing on the longer grass helps to maintain the field.

Did you know?

The farmers remove the animals from some of the fields in late winter and early in the year so the fields don't get churned up with too many animals walking or running on the land in wet weather, creating a lot of mud to appear in some places causing it to be poached. In the spring and summer, this allows the fields to rest and to have work done on them. Looking after the fields is essential. The farmers have to spread fertiliser over them to help with the growth of fresh grass. The chosen fields are then left for the grass to grow to produce hay and other animal feed while the animals graze on the rest of the fields.

Sometimes, other animals not from the farm may make a real mess of the fields without the farmers knowing. Suddenly, dirt piles can appear in all different shapes and sizes. Annoyingly, this can be done throughout a lot of the fields and can spread over a wide area! Have you ever seen this in fields or your garden?

Do you know what causes this? It's the moles!

Did you know?

Moles are small animals but can make an enormous mess when they dig. Moles spend nearly all their lives underground, below the surface of the fields or your garden. They spend their time burrowing and digging tunnels underground in which they live while travelling below the ground. The molehills you might see above the surface are caused by the moles digging below the ground, kicking and pushing up the dirt which comes through the top of the surface as they work hard to tunnel through the earth. Moles live on earthworms and many other insects they will find underground. You will see these molehills covering the fields, especially around February and March time and into spring, as the moles are desperately hunting for food after the winter months.

In spring, when the weather is warmer and dryer, and the fresh grass has grown, the first cut of grass is usually taken straight from the field. This is known as making silage for the farmers who have cows. This can be done several times each year through the seasons. The cut grass will be lifted off the field straight after it has been cut using a silage chopper machine. The grass is sucked up into the huge shoot of the chopper and then blown out of the top into a trailer which runs along beside it, pulled by a tractor. When the trailer is full, the tractor takes it and dumps its load into the silage pit where it is stored for feeding the animals later in the year. As one tractor and full trailer drive away, another tractor and empty trailer must be ready to move straight beside the chopper, and this carries on until all the silage has been cut from the fields and put into the silage pit. This can carry on late into the night, especially if the weather is due to change. The farmers will want to get all the silage cut and stored in the pit before rain arrives.

In this pit, the loose-cut grass is tightly packed into the space to the top and then covered well with a waterproof tarpaulin sheet tied tightly to the sides. Then, heavy tyres are usually laid on top of the pit to help keep the cover down. As the grass ferments in the pit, it turns into silage, and the farmers use this for feeding the cows later in the year as part of their feed. It looks very different when it is taken out later in the year, as seen in the picture at the top of the next page.

The cut of grass, which usually starts in the early summer months when you can see the green grass growing much higher and thicker in the fields where there are no animals, is for different types of feed for animals. This cut is generally used to make hay or haylage.

In these fields, you will see the tractor and machine cutting the grass and then leaving it lying on the ground for a while, depending on whether the farmer is making hay or haylage. The cut grass will then get turned over if needed, with a different machine called a grass tedder that gets fitted to the back of the tractor. This machine turns the cut grass over as many times as needed, depending on the weather conditions.

For making hay, this machine can fluff the grass up and turn it over as many times as needed so the air can get through the cut grass to dry out more.

Later, the grass tedder will be changed to a rake fitted to the back of the tractor to gather up the cut grass in the fields, putting it into rows ready for the baler machine. The tractor tows this machine as it takes the grass in and makes it into round or square bales, which can be of various sizes and shapes in different farms.

While in the field, the cut grass is fed into the baler through the bottom of the machine as it drives along with the tractor. Once the bale has been made, it rolls back out of the machine onto the ground, ready to be collected by the next machines. Sometimes, you will see hay bales sitting in the field for a few days or longer during a good harvest weather season until all the fields nearby have been worked. Then, they are lifted. The farmers will work late into the night at harvesting times to complete the job and make a good supply.

If you have been to an agricultural show, you may have sat on one of the small square bales, which are sometimes used to make seating for children around the show rings for the pet animals. A cover would be put over this for you because the bales are very itchy to sit on.

For haylage, this grass is cut earlier than for hay. It is left to wilt on the ground for a short period of time rather than being allowed to dry out and will only be turned over once or twice. It will be baled with moisture still in the grass, as it will be wrapped in several layers of plastic by a wrapping machine to keep the moisture content high and the grass fresh. This haylage will then be fed to the animals later in the year. You may see these big haylage bales outside on the farm where they are generally stored. They are usually easy to spot in their black, green, or white coloured wraps. Sometimes, you might see the farmers drawing smiley faces or cartoon characters on their bales at the farm or in the fields so passers-by can enjoy seeing them.

When the hay is made from the grass, it is cut at a later stage of growth and is turned quite a few times on the ground to allow it to dry out before being baled, either round or square. The round ones have netting wrapped around them several times, while the square ones have twine wrapped over them at different points to keep them together. The hay bales will then be stored inside a barn under cover to keep them dry and out of the bad weather.

The farmer can then hopefully feed most of their animals with the bales. This is an excellent way to supply their own feed for the animals' diet, which helps reduce the cost of feeding their animals. Other farmers will grow the above crops and sell them to people for feeding their animals, or contractors will buy them from the farmers to sell in different places.

The fields supply a good source of food for the animals, and other fields will have good grass growing in them for natural grazing. Usually, the animals will move from field to field when the grazing fields get low on grass. That's why you will notice them in different places at different times of the year or when the fields are being put to another use.

Chapter 3

Food For Thought

You may notice other fields in the countryside are sown with different crops, and some fields may look more golden in colour rather than green. There are a variety of straw fields later in the year in which, after the straw is grown, the seeds (usually barley, oat, or wheat) are taken off the long stems by the combined harvester. These are then collected and put into store to be used or sold later in the year. These seeds might be used for animal feed on their own or mixed with other animal feeds. They are also sold for a wide variety of food uses for human consumption in the food chain. Once these are ready, they will be sold to the suppliers, who will produce them.

Did you know?

Wheat

A good few acres of a wheat straw field could give enough wheat to add to flour for baking bread, cereal, drinks, and other food sources, including animal feeds. A field of just one acre of wheat could produce enough flour to make over 3000 loaves of bread for us to eat and maybe have a slice of toast with your breakfast.

Barley Seeds

Barley seeds are added to lots of different produce. You can find it in lots of our foods, including breads, breakfast cereals, puddings, porridges, stews and soups such as Scotch broth, barley water, beer, and other alcoholic drinks. 70% of the world's barley is used for animal feed.

Oats

Oats are used for a variety of food, including porridge, biscuits, cereal bars, and animal feeds.

Straw Stems

Straw stems are cut and used for various things, such as animal bedding and food. The straw can also be used to make a lot of different types of straw baskets and hats by weaving the straw. It can also be used to make building materials.

Some eco-friendly houses have been built using straw for insulation in the walls in the Scottish Highlands. One of these was constructed approximately fifteen years ago and used 500 bales of straw. In 2023, a house was being built using straw bales just off the path from the Trossachs Holiday Park near Aberfoyle.

It's interesting when looking at these kinds of houses because you would never know that the straw is inside the walls insulating them.

Did You Know?

Straw was used for insulation many years before the modern form of insulation was created.

Straw is one of the most sustainable forms of insulation and the cheapest.

Other crops grown from the ground that you may see in the countryside include a huge selection of potatoes, carrots, leeks, corn, turnips, cabbage, cauliflower, and beetroot. Specially selected places might also have a variety of fresh fruit. You may have even been to one of Scotland's many pick-your-own fruit farms and enjoyed finding and picking your own.

If the fruit is not sold directly from the farms or other outlets, it is then transported around the country by our farmers, lorry drivers, and transport companies to the places being prepared for sale before entering the shops and supermarkets.

You might be attracted to a field full of a crop growing that has a strong, bright yellow colour, but this should be avoided at all times.

This is rapeseed. When the pretty yellow flowers blossom in the fields, they have a very high erucic acid content, which is harmful to animals and humans. Rapeseed is highly poisonous to dogs, causing terrible wounds to their skin if they run through this crop, and can also affect their breathing. Humans who have sensitive airways might also find their breathing is affected.

The high acid content of rapeseed can be used in the production of lacquers, detergents, and plastic.

As you can see, the farmers and their work on the land and with their animals are very important to us all. Farmers play an essential part in where some of our foods begin. With the care of the land and the production of crops carefully chosen and selected to grow, and with the breeding and producing of animals, without them, the food chain would be in a poor supply of produce.

Chapter 4

Food Beginnings

Did you know?

Some of the animals the farmers have are kept for grazing the fields or for other purposes and breeding, but they also provide a food source for human consumption in the food chain.

Cows

The easiest ones to think of are the dairy cows. Only female cows produce and supply us with fresh milk. There are quite a few breeds, but the popular one you might see in the fields is the black and white cow, the Holstein Friesen.

Cows are very good at producing milk. A good milking cow can produce roughly 30 to 35 litres daily. This means over a week, one cow could produce 245 litres of milk. If you think of this amount, it could easily fill a standard five-foot bath in your house.

In the dairy parlour, once the cow has been milked, the milk goes into a refrigerated tank until it is collected shortly afterwards. Then, it is taken from the farmer's tank by the milk tankers, who take it to the processing factories to prepare it for delivery to shops and supermarkets for sale. You can then see it in the bottles or milk cartons in your house.

Some farmers still like the old way milk used to be delivered to your door by the milkman. Some large dairy farms that produce and process their own milk still deliver it to houses, usually in glass bottles that were used long before the plastic and cartons were introduced. These bottles are returned to the farmers when they make their next delivery.

Selected calves from these dairy cows go for milk production roughly from about two and a half years old. Other calves may be kept or sold.

The beef cattle shown here are quite happy in their field for grazing and are a mixture of Charolais, and Limousin bullocks roughly about fifteen months old.

If the calf is being bred for meat, it will eventually go to the market to be sold, and it will then go for beef into the food chain from roughly two to two and a half years old up to three years old. From birth, the calf could be sold several times to different farmers before entering the food chain. The more mature cattle go to market at various ages.

The markets have many pens and rings where the animals will go for the different sale types. Any animals sold for meat end up in an abattoir, where livestock animals go to be slaughtered and processed for meat.

Meat sold by farmers for food consumption must go through a reputable butcher to prepare the meat for sale to the public, whether from farms, markets, or shops. This makes it safe for you to eat and provides good quality meat for us all.

All the beef cattle that are bred and produced for meat for the food chain provide us with some good beef meat such as hamburgers, steaks, sirloin, brisket, rib, loin, and more different cuts.

Sheep

Sheep are another common farm animal, and the Scottish blackface sheep are often seen in the fields.

Jacob sheep, which are brown and cream, are also popular and can be easily spotted while grazing the land.

The wool clipped off the sheep can be sold to produce various things, including wool, clothing, thread, and rugs.

As you put your clothes on, have you ever thought of the sheep this way, from the sheep on the land to the clothing in your hand?

The sheep also have different uses. They are great animals for grazing the fields, but some sheep and lambs are bred and produced for meat.

You will notice that the lambs are usually born near March or April when you can see many of them in the fields with the other sheep. Some of them will be sold later in the year, going into the food chain to supply good quality meat, such as sausages, chops, stewing meat, and lots of other cuts of meat. The more mature sheep are sold at different times throughout the year. Here, you can see a good selection of meat from the various animals in this meat chart.

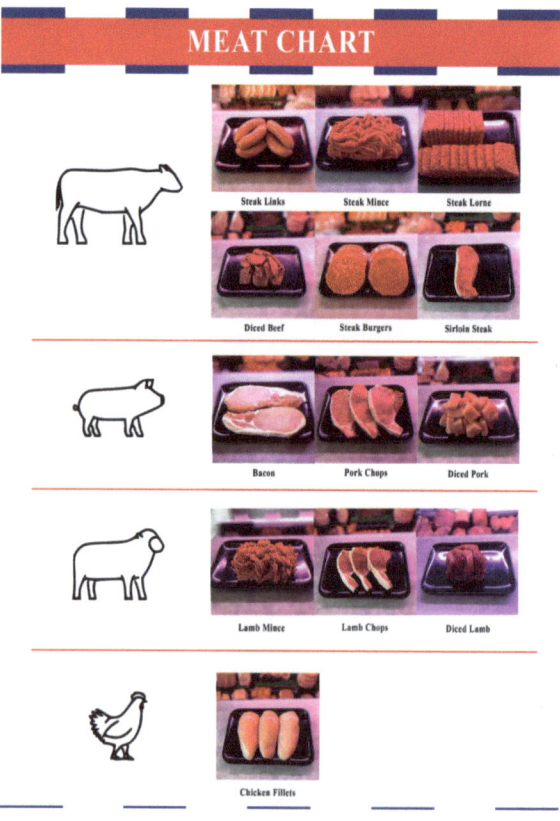

Chickens

Chickens are kept on some farms for the production of meat and eggs. Some chickens are kept in commercial production facilities, but lots of people keep chickens in the countryside at their homes for their own eggs to be produced.

There is a wide variety of breeds of chickens. Probably the most popular would be the Isla Brown breed, which is brown in colour.

The caged chickens are either kept in cages or enclosed areas where they are looked after. They don't have any space to roam about or have no access to the outdoor space, but hopefully, this will change in the future!

Free-range chickens are free to go outside and roam around. It is their natural instinct as it gets dark to hide from predators, so they will be kept in enclosed pens and chicken coops during the night to protect them and keep them safe from the birds, foxes, badgers, and other prowling animals that might attack them. This also makes it easier to find and collect the eggs, which are laid in the early morning, and also keeps them safe from the birds and animals eating the eggs before the farmer collects them.

Being free-range chickens, they are outside after laying in the morning, where they can roam freely around the land. This method of keeping hens does not harm their normal behaviour.

Along with the chicken food given to them, they have a great variety of natural food sources to eat from the fields or ground as they roam around outside their house coop. The free-range hens can peck at and eat whatever they can from the grass, soil, or trees, including worms, bugs, and flies.

Other chickens that are kept in a confined space need extra feeding. This way, the eggs they lay provide us with a good source of protein and vitamin D, which helps your immune system when eaten and is good for your health.

Eggs can be used in many ways, or they can be eaten on their own or with other foods and are ideal for mixing in for baking. They play a big part in our daily food, whether they are bought from farms, shops, or other places.

Notice the different colours in these eggs from various types of hens.

Did you know?

Adult female chickens are called hens. Depending on their breed, the hens can usually start laying their first egg at about 20 weeks old, but some may not start laying until about six months old. They will then typically keep laying eggs every day. However, their laying slows down or could even stop when the seasons change to autumn and winter with shorter days and colder weather. In their first year of laying, you could expect over 200 eggs from hens that are well-fed and producing well. They may continue to lay until they are about two to three years old when their egg production will slow down.

For commercial production places with hens, as they start to slow down laying, they would then be put into the food chain for their meat as they count on good production numbers to keep supplying the eggs for sale. This is where you get your good chicken meat. Smaller places or people who keep them at their homes could let them continue laying a few eggs over time.

Sometimes, eggs will be left with what we call the brood hens, who sit on the eggs once laid to hatch them into baby chicks. If there are a lot of brood hens, they will usually be housed in different coops. Some chickens are specifically bred from choice for different reasons, especially if they will be used for breeding later.

Animals are kept for different reasons by farmers and people. Along with other animals, there is a lot of work that goes into choosing the correct type of animal required for their breed, character, and nature of the animals to be kept, especially if for breeding purposes.

Many farmers and people know exactly what they want and will go out of their way to select the best quality animal to produce the best of their choice, whether for horses, ponies, sheep, cows, or a wide variety of animals.

France Farm in Gartocharn near the beautiful Loch Lomond is well known for breeding and producing top-quality Highland Cattle over the years for the showing ring at the selected Highland Cattle Society shows. One of the cows is shown here with her special name.

Shonag 3rd of Gartocharn is a three-year-old female Highland cow. She is the third calf born from her mother, and that is where her name comes from.

Shonag is lovely and quiet, and she goes to livestock shows to be shown by someone leading her. Before the shows, she has to get ready to be shown at her best. Shonag loves to be pampered and handled; she gets washed all over her body, blow-dried, and brushed. Her horns are filed and polished before going into the show ring. This is probably just the same as you like to get all ready to go out somewhere nice.

Shonag loves having children visit her while they are shopping at the farm shop with the adults.

Shonag is expecting a baby calf in early 2025, but you would never know this by looking at her.

Did you know?

Shonag is a Gaelic name.

In Highland cattle, the females have long, thin horns that curve up, just like Shonag's.

The male bulls have horns that are shorter and thicker and point forward, with only a slight curve.

When showing in the rings at the shows, the horns are very important and must be in top condition while being judged for the overall appearance and condition of the Highland cattle.

Here, you can see a Champion Rosette won by Shonag at one of the Highland Cattle Society Showing Shows. This is one of many won by these fantastic, bred Highland cattle from France Farm over the years.

Maybe you have seen shows, or if you visit agricultural shows, you can see the different animals in the rings, especially if you see the Royal Highland Show at Ingliston near Edinburgh in the summer, where all the animals have first to compete at other shows to qualify to be there, along with other big shows around the country.

Did you know?

There are a lot of things that you may come across through time that have similar titles and names, but they are quite different.

For example, below is a bird's-eye view picture of one of the farmers' markets, The Caledonian Marts Ltd in Stirling.

This is one of many auction farmers' markets where different agricultural animals go to be bought or sold, as mentioned earlier. The farmers and people will take the animals to be sold either to different people or to different farmers. They can purchase other cows and sheep there, too.

There will be different days and times for the different sales at different markets, like this one, for when the animals enter the auction ring.

The different markets will also have different days for selected animals to be sold for going into the food chain, and they will start their journey here or may also be sold at other places.

There are a lot of auction markets around the country where the farmers will take their animals to be sold, and they may be looking to buy other ones.

Another type of market known as the farmers' market is similar to this.

Here we have as an example of one, France Farm, Gartocharn.

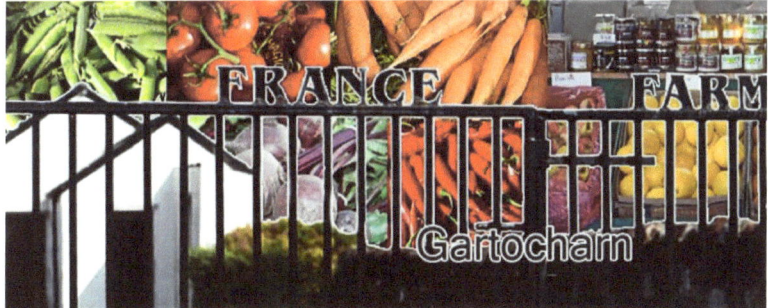

France Farm Shop is a family-run business based in the village of Gartocharn near the beautiful Loch Lomond. Renowned for the quality and freshness of their fruit and vegetables, they also stock a range of other locally sourced Scottish produce.

Throughout the year, the Farm shop has a glorious array of salads, herbs, fruit, and vegetables, including a selection of in-season locally grown potatoes, summer fruits, and

Scottish free-range eggs. You can also find Stornoway black pudding, bacon, hams, Highland butchered meat, locally produced dairy products, and a wide variety of other produce.

Did you know?

The McKechnie family from France Farm has supplied the finest fruit and vegetables to both retail and wholesale customers since 1959.

Farmers' markets similar to this are also held at different times throughout the year, at various places, and some farmers may hold them weekly, like France Farm.

You can also buy a wide selection of fresh produce at these markets, including fresh vegetables, fruit, eggs, and meat.

The fresh produce is carefully selected from our hard-working farmers.

Chapter 5

Caring for the environment

A long with Shaki and the other farmers taking care of the land and the countryside for the animals to graze and live on, there is always plenty of work to do. This includes looking after the environment and helping the planet in their daily land management and care. Leaving part of the edges in the fields for wild grazing to encourage wildlife and hibernation is a good way to attract different species and help with their reproduction. Insects are especially important for our planet.

Along with the different things taken off and out of the fields, some farmers plant trees around their land because trees are a natural source and help to keep the air clean. Trees make it fresh for us to breathe in the air as they kill off the toxins which enter our normal daily air.

Did you know?

Every day, one huge tree can take in gallons of nutrients dissolved in the soil. It converts this up to the top of its branches and through its leaves, releasing pure oxygen into the air. So, if we can plant lots of trees to be taken care of and replaced, it will make a big difference to the environment.

Trees also give natural shelter to animals and wildlife in the fields and countryside. You can sit under the branches of a tree to get a nice, shaded spot from the sunshine on a lovely summer's day.

You will notice the changes in the countryside throughout the year with the different seasons by the colours, nature, and animals you see.

Spring is always a precious time with the growth of colour and fresh bloom. The young cherry blossom trees we planted the previous year in late summer (as shown in our book of Sesky's Farmyard Friends) were growing and producing a lot of bright pink and red flowers in their first spring.

The picture of an old cherry blossom tree on the next page shows you the twisted trunk as it slowly turns through time, following the sun.

Like a wide variety of trees planted in and around the countryside, they all display lovely colours throughout most of the year as they change throughout the seasons.

Some trees stay green all year round, like the fir tree, which never loses its colour, and you can easily spot them in autumn and winter. These are known as evergreen.

The trees that lose their colour and leaves, and some lose their fruit in the autumn and winter, are called deciduous. As you can see in the picture, they look very bare throughout late autumn and winter.

A common deciduous tree is an oak tree from which the acorns fall off in the autumn, followed by the leaves in the winter until the tree is bare. Although the acorns that fall off look nice, they are poisonous to horses, ponies, cattle, sheep, and dogs if eaten by them and can be fatal if eaten in large quantities. Raw acorns can also be toxic to humans if eaten.

There are a lot of deciduous trees, including fruit trees like the apple tree, where the fruit and leaves will fall off as the seasons change.

They will regain their colour and growth in the spring when the weather turns warmer, and new shoots are grown, sprouting to the sky again.

Did You Know ?

This oak tree is slightly different; the Oak Tree Inn at Balmaha is near beautiful Loch Lomond. It is a very popular restaurant and bar, with a handy shop, and one selling coffee and ice cream. This family-run business has a fantastic oak tree, which is over 500 years old and stands in the corner position of its grounds.

Not far away from here is a very popular oak tree that looks quite small compared to others. It is known as the 'Lone Tree'. This oak tree sits in Milarrochy Bay on the Banks of Loch Lomond. This is the most photographed tree in Scotland, capturing the hearts of everyone who sees it with its presence in the beautiful Loch Lomond.

Did you know?
Going Greener

Some trees are grown specifically by the forestry department, and some are cut down through time for a variety of things, with their permission. The wood from the trees can be recycled and used to make all kinds of things, even furniture. Also, the wood cuttings can be put to many different uses, one of which is to be made into wood pellets for burning. This is a way of helping to save the environment and helps to reduce air pollution, making it kinder for our health. They can also be used to burn in boilers instead of fuel to produce energy savings. The wood shavings can also be used for animal bedding. Some people also use woodchips for resurfacing garden paths, and laying them on top of a plastic cover on the path stops the weeds from coming through the woodchips.

Some of the pencils you use and hold have also been made from these trees, so as you can see, trees are very important to our planet.

Chapter 6

Amazing nature

Along with the different colours of the trees, fields, surroundings and many different animals, the countryside is an astonishingly beautiful place to experience. From the changes of life with the newborn animals throughout the seasons and the farmers' never-ending work on the land with the crops and fields, to the colour and smell of freshly cut grass lingering in the air as they go about their harvesting, spending time in the countryside you can just take it all in. It's a place where nothing seems the same from one day to another, and there will always be something for you to see, discuss and smile about. In the countryside, you will get the chance to see the different wild animals as they tend to roam about here as it is quieter than the towns and cities.

If you take time to stroll and look, you can see the magical work from even the smallest things glistening in the sun or on a frosty morning. The incredible workings of the spider's web can be seen easily and will astonish you.

These can be attached to whatever the spiders find as they work their way around to make the most fantastic design, and this little spider cleverly weaves them together.

Squirrels

If you want to catch a glimpse of the squirrels fast at work, your eyes must be wide open and alert. They run about the ground or scamper high up into the trees, fetching and carrying food and anything they can to make themselves safe  and out of harm's reach, using the trees for shelter. Sometimes, squirrel boxes might even be put up for them, which helps save this animal. The red squirrel, as seen here, is a popular species of tree squirrel, but they are a lot rarer than the grey squirrel.

Roe Deer

If you're lucky, the sudden appearance of the roe deer is such a sight to see as they wander about, as if tiptoeing across the fields. Then, if they are startled or frightened, they will take off and run across the fields, jumping the fences or hedges with their elegant body covering a good height in the air as they go from field to field, making the jump and flight look effortless. Their natural instinct is to run from whatever frightens them to protect themselves and disappear into the covered tree and bush areas where they will feel safe.

The Pheasant

Another animal seen in the trees and bushes where it can hide from predators is the pheasant, especially later in the year once it has grown and matured.

The male pheasant is easy to spot, with his head of beautiful colours. A blue and green neck and red around the eyes dominate his head as he proudly stands tall with a golden brown body and sharp tail, looking very proud of himself.

The female pheasant is smaller, with a lighter brown spotted body, which makes it harder to see her between the trees and bushes as she blends in with the colour as a natural camouflage for her. Sometimes, she can sit on the fence post unspotted until you come quite near, when she suddenly screeches and flies into the air, frightening you or any other animals.

Rabbits

You might also spot a few rabbits running around the ground because the pheasant has frightened them. They will have been hiding in the longer grass, trying not to be noticed as you approached.

Field Mouse

Another very hard animal to spot is the field mouse.

Although this one has amazingly been captured here, tucking into his food, quite unaware that he has been seen.

These are very clever animals at hiding and keeping still in the countryside, avoiding danger or anything suspicious. Their colours blend in with the scenery, making it easy to move around, but others may be watching.

Chapter 7

Birds of Prey

The wild birds of prey, with their sharp eyes and ears, may spot the field mice and rabbits quite easily. These birds are very special to see flying around. You will not always see them, but it is quite a sight if you're lucky enough. Out and about in the countryside is the ideal place to catch a view of some of these wonderful birds where it is generally a bit quieter than in the town, where they would be disturbed and fly away and hardly be noticed. In the countryside, they can be seen flying around, and then they suddenly swoop down from the sky on their prey to hunt, catch, and feed on them.

Did you know?

Birds of prey (also known as raptors) pursue other animals for food. The term 'raptor' derives from the Latin 'rapio', meaning to seize or take by force.

Mice and rabbits are the main food source for birds of prey, but they will easily hunt for other animals.

Throughout the world, there are more than 500 species of raptors.

Raptors eat the whole of their prey, meaning they eat the fur, feathers, bones, and teeth of their meal, along with everything else, although the bones and fur are hard for them to digest.

The fastest bird of prey is the peregrine falcon, which can reach speeds up to 242 mph.

Owls

Not all owls make the distinct twit twoo noise that we think they do. The only owl in the world to make that noise is the most common owl species in the UK, the tawny owl, as seen below in its time of flight.

The other most widely distributed owl in the world is the barn owl. The global population of these birds is around 10 million. They can mostly be found nesting in derelict buildings or in hollows of trees and in an old barn on the farm or countryside where it is quiet. The owl will usually be high up in the corner where it will have made its nest, hoping it won't be disturbed too much there. It will stay here quite happily unless disturbed, then it may nest somewhere else, but each year, they usually like to return to where they have been before.

It is common to see owls in the animal barns up in the corner, and it is not bothered about the animals on the ground. Sometimes, later at night, the barn owl can be spotted swooping down and catching the field mice that wander in and go through the hay bales and straw, making them an easy catch and dinner for the owl whilst it stays safe.

The barn owls will eat mice, shrews, and voles. Being completely silent in flight, they can appear suddenly.

Owls have excellent hearing because of their asymmetrical ears; one ear is higher than the other, which means they hear their prey before seeing them. Their habitat is grassland, wetlands, and farmlands, where they will fly above long grass and crops in a figure-of-eight motion to pinpoint their prey. Most of them will hunt at different times of the night.

Sometimes, while walking in the countryside, you will see an owl suddenly fly off the trees or fence posts where it has been sitting, watching for prey.

In the picture on the next page, you can see the barn owl in flight.

Kestrels

The Common Kestrel was once the most common bird of prey species in the UK. Sadly, their numbers have fallen by half since the 1970s because of the loss of habitat and nesting sites and the use of pesticides to kill rodents. The loss of these  birds has increased since 2021, with many kestrel carcasses being found in the wild that have died from secondary poisoning because rodents are a kestrel's main diet.

Kestrels are known for hovering and are mostly seen over hedgerows, grass verges, and along the sides of roads and waterways. With extremely sharp eyesight, kestrels can spot a beetle from 50 meters away. They can even see ultraviolet light, which is invisible to the human eye. This means they can detect the urine trails left by rodents on the ground, helping the birds locate their prey. Shown here, you can see the sharp eyes of the kestrel as it sits in the bush, awaiting its next victim.

The Common Buzzard

In Scotland, the buzzard is sometimes called the tourist eagle because many visitors mistake it for the larger golden eagle.

The common buzzard is the UK's most common bird of prey. They can survive in most habitats, including woodland farmland and moorland, and may even be seen in urban areas if there is sufficient green space. Buzzards are opportunistic predators and will take a wide variety of prey. Small rodents, such as voles and mice, are commonly eaten. They can also take prey as large as rabbits or as small as earthworms. This is not so good if they are about the gardens and see pets or the free-range chickens, as they could become victim to the buzzard. They will also scavenge on roadkill, where you can see them while driving. This flexible diet allows the buzzard to survive in a variety of habitats.

These are just a few of the birds of prey that you might see in the countryside.

Did you know?

While the wild birds of prey that fly overhead are free and belong to no one, some birds belong to centres like the one in this picture.

The Loch Lomond Bird of Prey Centre is a popular visitor attraction beside the Bonnie banks of Loch Lomond. It has evolved over the years to become one of the country's premier bird of prey centres.

The natural and idyllic setting provides a relaxing atmosphere for both visitors and birds. The high standard of accommodation, cleanliness, and welfare ensures the well-being of the resident birds in their charge.

This book features only some of their birds, but in the centre, you can see many more types of birds of prey. Although still able to live freely, you can see the birds up close in their living environment and learn how they are being looked after. You can also watch flying demonstrations with these magnificent birds at the centre in the flying area within a managed woodland. While listening to the commentary from their specialist handlers, you will learn about their daily care and lives.

With special permission from the farmers and landowners, these birds are flown out in the countryside on several occasions to let them use their natural instinct to hunt and fly from distances with their handlers and use the sky as their own while demonstrating their skill of flying and returning to their handler at chosen times. This is a magnificent achievement for the handlers who put in a massive amount of work to build up a partnership between them and the birds, which can be seen at all times. With daily flying shows, walk rounds, a learning zone, educational days, and a whole lot more things to offer, it is a fantastic day out to mix in with your walk in the countryside or the beautiful Loch Lomond.

CHAPTER 8

Recycling to Help the Planet

Out in the countryside, you will notice a lot of outbuildings and sheds beside the farmhouses or standing alone. Not only are these used to store feed, hay, straw, or machinery to keep it dry and safe, but some of these buildings can also be used for housing all different types of animals, including the milking parlour for milking the cows. Other buildings have several uses at various times of the year.

In the wintertime, many animals are kept inside for a few months. They will be brought in off the fields and kept inside, dry, warmer, and safe from severe weather conditions as winter worsens. This also helps to maintain the fields, so they are not getting into too much of a mess with the wet weather and with the animals running around on them, poaching the ground, and causing a lot of mud. With the grass getting less and having no feed value in it at this time of year, hay or haylage must be put out for the animals, and if the fields are in poor conditions, this can be very hard to do, causing a lot more work, and a lot of food waste.

When the animals are indoors, it makes everything a bit easier. This also allows for the good care of their feet, and it's easier to keep an eye on their diet and weight. However, being inside creates extra work because more mucking out has to be done keeping their bedding fresh and clean, but this saves the farmers a lot of work in repairing the damaged fields and lets the fields rest for a while.

Did you know?

Recycling has great advantages for the environment.

Poo from the animals and cows housed in sheds is known as dung, and this creates excellent manure.

The cattle or animals in the large sheds produce a lot of dung and urine droppings daily, which need cleaning out, along with their dirty, soiled bedding. The farmer builds dung piles in the yard, which will get bigger and rot over time. A lot of work is involved in looking after the dung heap, but this can eventually be spread out across the fields as a natural source of fertiliser.

While the dairy cows are in the dairy sheds, they have pens where they sleep, but walking around in the barn, they also drop dung and urine waste on the corridor floors. This all gets pulled along the floor with the scraper machines that go along the floors at different set times, and it is dragged to the slats, where it gets pushed down into the tank in the ground. From here, it gets pumped into the slurry tank, where it is collected and stored before being spread on the farmland.

When you're out walking or driving in the countryside, especially at the start of spring, you can smell that strong manure that lingers in the air as the farmers start to feed the fields for the new growth of grass. You can smell it at different times of the year when it is put onto the fields again to help with the re-growth of grass, as the grass is eaten down bare by the animals or is cut for the silage, hay or haylage seasons.

Re-using the slurry as a natural source of fertiliser is great for the ground as it is a fantastic, effective, and rich fertiliser, as it feeds the soil and also helps to reduce the vast amounts of chemical fertilisers and sprays used on the fields, which would then go into the air. It also reduces the amount of fertilisers the farmers have to buy, which is a great way to look after the land and help our environment. It also goes towards reducing the farmers' high cost of fertiliser use.

Did you know?
You can recycle rainwater!

The rainwater running off the farm buildings and sheds can be collected and diverted from the roofs and guttering before it goes down into the drains. The rainwater can then flow into large water-holding containers, giving plenty of fresh drinking water for the animals or washing out the sheds and floors, watering crops and plants, and has many other uses such as helping to wash out buckets, bins or the dirty trailer floors.

Re-using the rainfall and helping to reduce the amount of rainwater that falls off the roofs into the ground can help reduce the chance of flooding in severe weather situations by redirecting the water from the drains. With some farmers making their own water recycling systems, this reduces the pressure on the main water drains and sewage system while at the same time making a convenient natural water supply anywhere when needed with no water pipes being laid into the ground to supply the water.

Recycling rainwater can also save money by reducing the amount of water usage from the main water supply we pay for. Having that extra water collected and available when there is a shortage of water in very hot weather conditions could be very handy, especially if there is a hose pipe ban and water usage cuts put into force, or water mains trouble that pops up with burst pipes. Our farmers are always thinking ahead of all ways to keep their workload going in ways that benefit their animals, land, and all of us.

Some people with their own animals, horses, and ponies can quite easily divert the rainwater from the gutter into an

easy-to-make unit like the one shown here. My friend Iona made a great rainwater recycling collection unit to provide animals with drinking water.

Chapter 9

Horses and Ponies

Horses and ponies are often seen in the countryside or surrounding areas. Some of them have young foals wandering about in the fields with them at different times of the year, which is lovely to see.

Although horses, ponies, and other animals are lovely to look at, they can be very protective of their young or their own space, so wandering into the fields to pat these could be pretty dangerous. Horses and ponies are very flighty animals; if they get a sudden fright, it might result in something happening. You could get knocked over very suddenly if they start to run. It's always better and safer to look and admire their beautiful presence from a distance.

Some horses and ponies may have plenty of fields to graze in, whether part of a farm is used or from special yards that will keep them for people or, if some people are fortunate enough, they could have their own land and stables for them.

Horses and ponies have become very popular, creating a wonderful leisure time for people to have them as pets, working horses, or competition horses and ponies. Some are specially selected for breeding. You can see a lot of different breeds and sizes as you travel through the countryside.

Registered riding schools and trekking centres have an excellent selection of horses and ponies where you can pay to ride a horse or pony, either in the riding school or the countryside. This is a great experience, or even better if you can ride a horse or pony on a beach, that is an adventure not to be missed.

With my horse, Seskinore, known as Sesky, who I had for 28 incredible years, I experienced this on several occasions, and it is something I will never forget. She loved being on the farm and riding in the countryside, and of course, she loved eating the haylage, with that lovely smell that Shaki used to make for her off his fields.

Like all animals, horses and ponies can live to different ages. Sesky lived until she was 32, a very good age for a horse. She was still being ridden then and enjoying many a day riding in the fields and along the countryside paths and roads, which was exceptional for a horse of this age.

Sesky was an Irish draught cross-thoroughbred horse. When she was younger, she was a dapple-grey colour, but she turned white in her older years. This is known as a shade of grey in horses and ponies. You can see the dapple-grey colour when she was six years old. This is a picture of Sesky competing in the show jumping ring out in the countryside at a jumping show with me, probably about 1992.

Sesky started turning a lighter grey with a few dapple marks on her when she was about 15 years old. This is a picture of her when she was 28, and we had just returned from an excellent five-mile ride around the countryside.

Did you know?

Seskinore, Sesky's full name, is also a village in Northern Ireland. This is where she got her name, as she was born here.

Some horses, ponies, and other animals may change colour throughout their lives from the colour they were born. As mentioned previously, Sesky was a great example of this.

Horses and ponies are measured from the ground up to the top of their withers, the highest point of their back.

Sesky's height was 15.3hh. This means 15.3 hands high. The human hand has always been used to measure horses and ponies, going back to ancient times. One hand is equal to four inches. The diagram here shows how to measure them.

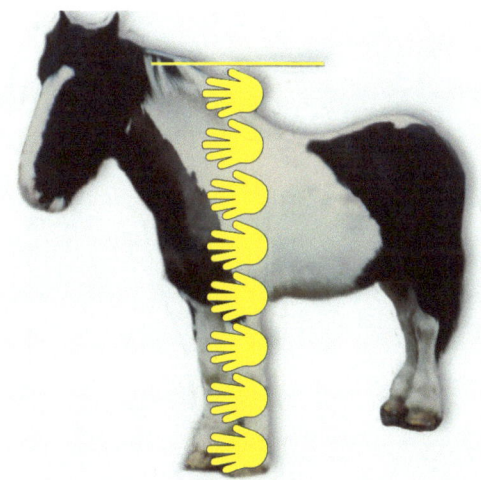

According to the Guinness World Records Book, in 2024, the tallest horse in the world was Sampson, who was 21.5h, just over seven feet two inches. He was a magnificent shire horse from back in 1846.

The Scottish-bred highland pony was originally bred to work on small farms in Scotland. Their height usually ranges from about 13hh to 14.2hh, but being a sturdy pony, they were ideal for working. They are also great riding ponies as they are good weight carriers for children and adults. These ponies are sure-footed on uneven ground, making them perfect for riding long distances over different terrain in the countryside.

Throughout the world, there are many heights, breeds, colours, shapes and sizes of horses and ponies, all living to different ages and all having varied lives. But they all have a beautiful presence wherever they are and create incredible partnerships with their owners.

Did You Know ?

Caledonia was a different type of horse.

This was the mechanical horse the British Horse Society used a good few years ago. Caledonia taught people to learn to ride and experience the different paces before they would go on a real horse or pony. Mechanical horses are also great for practising or getting back into riding after an accident or for someone just wanting to improve their balance and position without worrying about a live animal underneath them. This mechanical horse is a great asset to the riding sport for all.

Many places may have these mechanical horses, including racing yards, which are great for jockey training, as they can concentrate on balance without being on a lively horse while still practising.

I had the pleasure of having Caledonia, the mechanical horse and some British Horse Society staff accompany me when I was doing an event with my ponies from my riding school at the Loch Lomond Shores 10th-anniversary celebrations in 2012 Everyone had a great time trying out this mechanical horse that day, with many riding for their first time. As you can see in the picture, the mechanical horse is a good size for people to enjoy and practise on.

Did you know?

There is another Caledonia that is very different from the mechanical horse.

The old Latin name for Scotland is Caledonia.

The name Caledonia can be found in things about Scotland, and it is often used in poetry.

Chapter 10

Care and Attention.

Sometimes, we might think that we want to turn things into mechanical items, which might be easier, with just a bit of care looking after them, without all the running around and everything else. As Shaki, other farmers and people with animals know, having animals takes up much of your time, care and attention to detail to look after them. Shaki always says, "You can't take your eye off them for a minute, or something happens."

With the farmers doing a massive amount of work with their different animals and all the work on the land, they only know and appreciate that every second is needed and essential for getting things done. Sometimes, it feels like there are not enough hours in the day. But like others, whether breeding or buying animals and keeping them, whoever has them needs to look after them properly, and it all involves time, dedication, money, and a huge amount of hard work.

Looking after these animals is not an easy job for our farmers. As you can see, out in the countryside, there is a large turnover in animals throughout the year as the farmers change over their selected livestock. It takes a lot of work and care to look after these animals and maintain good health, weight, and condition during the changing seasons, especially in severe weather, and the farmers do their best to provide that.

They also supply other animals, not just their own, with a good food source and purchase other supplies elsewhere. They help hugely in providing us with many different kinds of food we eat and drink.

There is a saying that comes to mind;

No Farmers, no food!

We have a lot to be thankful to the farmers for not only keeping us supplied with many different types of food and fresh milk, but also providing and supplying this worldwide.

I think a huge thank you to Shaki and all the farmers and workers is needed, don't you?

Looking after animals, even as pets, takes a lot of work, as I'm sure many of you will already know. Even when we and the farmers do as much as possible for our animals, sometimes we need a bit of help when it comes to the animals for things outwith regular care and control.

Along with other qualified specialists who help with this, the vet is a very common person to be called upon at some point. Whether this is just for routine check-ups on any animal, injections needed for vaccinations, sickness or injury, or more serious things, they are on call all day and night. This sounds just like our farmers!

From time to time, a vet will need to visit the farms or different places, or smaller animals might have to be taken to the veterinary practice for care. Just like the farmers, dealing with a lot of different animals all the time, they never know what will lie ahead in the ordinary everyday world with animals.

Did you know?

Along with many different things needing to be addressed with the animals, there are also quite a few more specific treatments to be carried out.

Horses, ponies and other animals need to have their teeth checked. Just as you need to see a human dentist for this, animals must be seen by a qualified animal dentist or vet.

Small animals can usually be taken to the veterinary practice for this to be done, while the larger animals and farm animals will have the vet come out to the farms and yards for their treatment at different times throughout the year if needed or for check-ups.

Some animals need an injection to make them sleepy and drowsy, making examinations or treatment less stressful for them. Meanwhile, the vet or dentist checks their mouth and works on their teeth, making it much easier and safer for them both. Other animals don't bother when being looked at and are pretty happy for their mouth and teeth to be inspected and for treatment to be carried out.

Just like humans, animals need their teeth to help them eat properly and chew their food, so it is better for them as chewing food makes it easier to digest in the stomach.

There are special tools for this work to be carried out in the mouth for the teeth. The tools used for this are quite technical and should only be used by someone trained to do this work, or it could be extremely dangerous. For horses and ponies, vets have special equipment to open their mouths wide and keep them that way while working on their mouths, saving any unnecessary injury to the animal until the treatment is finished.

In this picture, you can see the whole inside of the horse's mouth from looking down inside while it is wide open for the teeth to be worked on and rasped to take off the sharp, jaggy edges of the teeth.

This is inside the mouth of a seven-year-old horse.

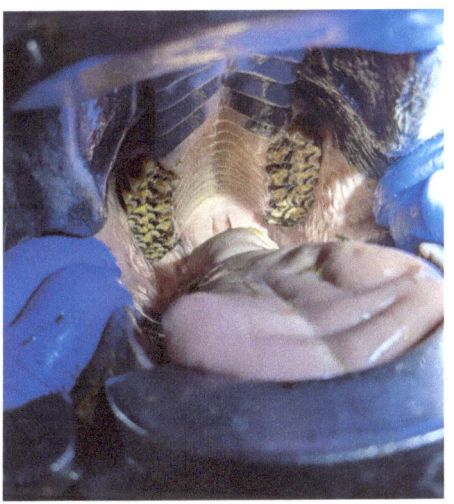

The vet was carrying out the work when this picture was taken. The horse had been sedated by a jag or injection to make her drowsy and sleepy so that the vet could carry out the work safely with no stress to either of them at the time of the work.

An adult horse has between 36-42 teeth. Ponies from five years old typically have about 38-44 permanent teeth.

Just like humans, if their teeth are not looked after, it could cause difficulty in eating and chewing the food.

Chapter 11

Countryside Code Tips

While it is beautiful to be out in the countryside enjoying this space, seeing the animals, and watching the farmers work the land, we also have to be aware of the dangers. While most animals can seem quiet and friendly at times, there is always that moment when the lovely, calm, friendly animal will turn into what seems like a dreadful evil monster, especially in the times of the year when they have their young with or near them. Your sudden appearance and presence alert them, and their natural instinct is to protect their young, especially if you enter the field or place to try to see or pat them. It is better never to do this in case of danger unless you are with the farmer or person who owns the animals and they give you permission to go in with them and your parents or guardians. Thinking ahead is always the best thing to do.

Being pack animals, animals will always run together, especially if frightened or startled. No matter who is there or if anything gets in their way, they will still run to somewhere they feel safe and out of harm's way.

The countryside will always be here for everyone to enjoy, including our animals, because of the hard-working farmers looking after their land and all of us trying to make a difference to keep it a beautiful place. We can all do our bit, as the farmers do, in looking after the environment. Every little counts to help save our planet and keep our world as beautiful as it is.

Did You Know ?

There are countryside code guides to help you while out in the countryside. Here are a few to give you an idea.

1- Enjoy the countryside, be safe, be seen, and always tell people where you are going. This is important for your safety.

2- Do not feed the animals.

3- Respect people's privacy.

4- Be aware of the natural hazards in the countryside.

5- Leave all the gates the way you find them.

6- Keep away from any work being carried out in fields, especially if the crops are being sprayed or there is farm machinery nearby.

7- Keep dogs on a lead near animals.

8- If you must go in a field to get to the other side, walk around the perimeter of the field, not over the crops. Look for warning signs first!

9- Some animals may be pregnant. Do not chase or frighten them or any other animals.

10- Report any signs of danger or accidents to the farmers or the animal owners.

11- Take all your rubbish home or put it in the bins to help the environment stay tidy and clean.

Enjoy, be safe, have fun!

THE END

A little saying you may like

What you Believe
You Can Achieve

ACKNOWLEDGEMENTS

I would like to once again for the third year running thank Kim & Sinclair from Indie Authors World for working with me and getting this book to the final stage and publication. Working with you both has been a pleasure each time your support and encouragement is greatly appreciated. Thanking Sinclair for your work in turning my draft into a beautiful book with all my wants and needs attended to with the special finishes.

Thanking my editor Debra Murphy for all your help and suggestions in such a quick return of work, we made the deadline I wanted our timing was incredible. It was a pleasure working with you for the first time.

Thanking Shaki for having to listen once again and having to put up with me asking the questions for the finer details for the book, without me giving too much away about it at the time as it was all being put together. The only thing is, this time Shaki you have been caught, not once but twice in here !

To Michael my son, a huge thank you for your help with the technical things again throughout this book and the dreaded phone calls you had to listen to from me when things went wrong. Although I am learning throughout each book !

To Gavin his friend, for the third year again a huge thank you. Although this time the front cover of this book was designed and put together by him exactly what I was wanting and I am delighted with it. Your help also in getting the pictures ready and into their digital files and your patience and understanding and advise was greatly appreciated. With the contribution of some of your photographs in the book which I needed you have helped to get this to the end. I cannot thank you enough. Also thanking Jeanette my friend for the lovely picture of Sesky out in the countryside near loch Lomond this always is a favourite of mine.

Thanking Stewart and Kevin from the Loch Lomond Bird of Prey centre, for working with me, and your inclusion in this book, with your pictures and the details given about these magnificent birds. Also, to everyone else who has contributed to this book and Big Daft cakes for that much needed dumpling picture. Without you all I would never have got here. This journey once again has been amazing.

Also, to everyone who has contributed to this book in your own way, family and friends for your encouragement, Caledonian Marts Ltd, France Farm, Sloan Butchers.

I guess that favourite saying comes to mind again,
"What you believe, you can achieve !"

About the Author

Janette created Dynamic Dream Books to share inspirational stories and experiences with people all over the world, young and old. Her 30 years of experience as a BHS Accredited Coach in horse riding and horse management has given Janette the opportunity to pursue her passion of teaching and training children and adults in the art of horses.

She was inspired to write by her horse, Sesky. Janette and Sesky were together for 28 amazing years, leading to many new opportunities in life for them both. In 2021 Janette followed her dream of writing and publishing her first book, *Good Girl, Sesky*, a story of true friendship which included helpful tips for horse management, perfect for the older reader.

She loved the publishing journey so much she couldn't wait to write her next book, her first children's book. *Sesky's Farmyard Friends*, Janette wanted to teach children about Sesky, her farmyard friends and introduction to farming in an easy and enjoyable way.

In this, the second book in her Dynamic Fun Learning Activity Book series, she gives children a more advanced understanding of life on a farm.

For more information visit:
www.dynamicdreambooks.co.uk